Remembering Our Black Trailblazer and Their *Legacies*

REMEMBERING OUR BLACK TRAILBLAZERS AND THEIR LEGACIES

Barbara A. Pierce

Remembering Our Black Trailblazers and Their Legacies by Barbara A. Pierce

This book is written to provide information and motivation to readers. Its purpose is not to render any type of psychological, legal, or professional advice of any kind. The content is the sole opinion and expression of the author, and not necessarily that of the publisher.

Copyright © 2018 by Barbara A. Pierce

All rights reserved. No part of this book may be reproduced, transmitted, or distributed in any form by any means, including, but not limited to, recording, photocopying, or taking screenshots of parts of the book, without prior written permission from the author or the publisher. Brief quotations for noncommercial purposes, such as book reviews, permitted by Fair Use of the U.S. Copyright Law, are allowed without written permissions, as long as such quotations do not cause damage to the book's commercial value. For permissions, write to the publisher, whose address is stated below.

Printed in the United States of America.

New Leaf Media, LLC
175 S. 3rd Street, Suite 200
Columbus, OH 43215
www.thenewleafmedia.com

To my mother Rita Mae Brown and my aunt Hattie Jones who remain beacons in many lives.

A special thanks to Barry Coleman for using his technical expertise to help complete this project, and Jean Hurst who always gives a supporting hand.

All images are from Wikipedia's public domain African American historical pictures.

TABLE OF CONTENTS

Introduction 1

Charles R. Drew	1904-1950	Physician, Blood Research Scientist	3
Mary McLeod Bethune	1875-1955	Educator	5
Lewis Howard Latimer	1848-1928	Electrician, Draftsman, Inventor	7
George Washington Carver	1864-1943	Agricultural Chemist, Teacher	9
Matthew Henson	1866-1955	Explorer, First to reach North Pole	11
Jesse Owens	1913-1980	Olympic Track Star	13
Rosa Parks	1913-2005	Mother of Civil Rights Movement	15
Granville T. Woods	1856-1910	Inventor, Electrical Engineer	17
Harriet Tubman	1821-1913	Underground Railroad Conductor	19
Benjamin Banneker	1731-1806	Astronomer, Mathematician, Editor	21
Bessie Coleman	1892-1926	Aviator	23
Althea Gibson	1927-2003	Tennis Player	25
Henry Ossawa Tanner	1859-1937	Artist	27
Marian Anderson	1897-1993	Concert singer	29
Jackie Roosevelt Robinson	1919-1972	Baseball Player	31
Langston Hughes	1902-1967	Poet, Author	33
Frederick Douglass	1817-1895	Freedom fighter, Statesman, Editor	35
Booker T. Washington	1856-1915	Educator	37
Thurgood Marshall	1908-1993	U. S. Supreme Court Justice	39
Martin Luther King, Jr.	1929-1968	Minister, Civil Rights Leader, Nobel Prize Winner	41

Ida B. Wells-Barnett	1862-1931	Civil Rights Advocate 43
Madame C. J. Walker	1867-1919	Businesswoman 45
James P. Beckwourth	1798-1866	Explorer, Pioneer 47
Sojourner Truth	1797-1883	Abolitionist, Orator 49
Danial Hale Williams	1856-1931	Surgeon (First successful heart surgery) 51
Percy Lavon Julian	1899-1975	Research Chemist 53
Jan E. Matzeliger	1852-1889	Inventor of Shoe-lasting Machine 55
Carter G. Woodson	1875-1950	Educator, Historian 57
Wilma Rudolph	1940-1994	Olympic Track Star 59
Ernest Everett Just	1883-1941	Research Cell Biologist 61
Phillis Wheatly	1753-1784	Poet 63
Paul Laurence Dunbar	1872-1906	Lyric Poet 65
Garrett A. Morgan	1877-1963	Inventor of Gas mask and Traffic Light 67
Elijah McCoy	1844-1929	Inventor, engineer 69

Bibliography 71

Additional Research recommendations 73

INTRODUCTION

The purpose of this book of brief biographies is to keep the memory of our black trailblazers alive, and to inspire further research on these extraordinary individuals. In spite of the racial divide and the negative sentiments that existed during their time, they pursued a path that improved the direct circumstances of many. It often came at a cost, nevertheless, adversity fueled their determination to make a difference. Their brave actions and significant contributions changed the course of history. The men and women mentioned in this book are but a fraction of those that were instrumental in bringing about that change.

Charles R. Drew
Born: June 3, 1904
Died: April 1, 1950

CHARLES R. DREW

Drew was born on June 3, 1904 to Richard and Nora Drew. He was the eldest of five children. His family lived quite modestly in the inner city of Washington, D. C. At twelve the boy took a newspaper route to contribute to his family's finances. Very early on his excellence in academics and sports were recognized. In elementary school, he won four swimming medals and later in high school, received an athletic scholarship to attend Amherst College. After college Drew's interest in chemistry and biology grew. He decided to become a doctor, but to do so he had to earn the money. After teaching school and studying on his own for two years, Drew was accepted at McGill University Medical School in Montreal, Canada where his research on blood began. Years later, Dr. Charles Drew initiated the first experimental blood banks. His research and experiments in the medical field led to the discovery that blood could be converted to plasma and preserved for later use during transfusions. In 1940, thousands of men, women and children injured during World War II benefited from this discovery. Dr. Drew was named director of the American Red Cross Project to collect and store the blood of donors. In 1941, he left the project to take a position as a professor of surgery and director of Freedman's Hospital when the U.S. War Department ordered that blood be segregated by race. Dr. Drew was furious that the Red Cross would go along with a theory that was not scientific. His extensive medical research indicated there was no "white" blood or "black" blood. Today, every hospital keeps plasma available in case there is a need for transfusions. Blood banks worldwide are memorials to the genius of Dr. Drew. He was killed in a car accident when he fell asleep at the wheel while returning from a speaking engagement in 1950.

Mary McLeod Bethune
Born: July 10, 1875
Died: May 18, 1955

MARY MCLEOD BETHUNE

Bethune was the daughter of former slaves. She was the youngest of the McLeod children and the only one born into freedom in 1875. Her family was very poor. Mary learned early what being black and poor meant for black folks, struggle and hardship, but the dream of getting an education flourished inside of her. In 1888, she was selected as a worthy candidate to receive a scholarship to further her education. She never forgot the help extended to her during those tough times. After getting married, she opened the Daytona Educational Industrial Training School for Negro Girls in 1904, the first of its kind. Its mission was to instruct young women in Christian values and personal self-reliance. And since the school was always in need of financial support Mary began knocking on doors, asking strangers for help, and organizing creative ways to raise the needed monies. Then in time, the school offered nursing and a more academic curriculum. Eventually the school merged with nearby Cookman Institute for Boys and later became a fully accredited coeducational college. As founder and president of the newly named school, Bethune- Cookman College, Mary McLeod Bethune continued her efforts to educate and improve the quality of life for young black youth. Her achievements won her the prestigious Spingarn Medal given by the NAACP. Throughout her life she worked as a civil rights and women's rights leader. The educator also served as a special advisor on minority affairs in the White House to Presidents Franklin D. Roosevelt and Harry S. Truman. And during the Great Depression in the 1930s Mary McLeod Bethune was called by President Franklin Roosevelt to head a special program to help keep thousands of poor black children in school. Her skills were recognized and used by Roosevelt and other presidents as well.

Lewis Howard Latimer
Born: September 4, 1848
Died: December 11, 1928

LEWIS HOWARD LATIMER

Latimer was born in Chelsea, Massachusetts on September 4, 1848. His parents George and Rebecca Latimer were once slaves in Virginia before escaping in 1842. Lewis, the youngest of their four children was the only child born free. During his school years he often helped out in his father's barbershop and other jobs. When his father abandoned the family in 1858, they were left in financial difficulty. Lewis tried to help his mother support the family by trying various jobs without much success. Eventually the lad enlisted in the Union Navy during the Civil War. He served almost a year until he was discharged. Later, a bit of good fortune intervened. Latimer was hired as an office boy with Croshy, Halsted, and Gould, a reputable patent drafting firm. While working for the firm Latimer acquired an interest in drafting. He taught himself mechanical drawing and drafting by observing the work of the draftsmen at the office and then practicing their techniques at home. When the firm recognized Latimer's talent, he received a promotion to draftsman in 1873 and later, head draftsman with a substantial increase in his salary. Over the course of Latimer's career as a draftsman, his work impressed many, particularly Alexander Graham Bell who hired him to draft the blueprints for the first telephone in 1876. Another interested scientist was Thomas Edison. Lewis Latimer went to work in the legal department of Edison Electric Light Company in 1890, which has since become the General Electric Company. Latimer's interest in electric lighting led to his finding a way to make light bulbs last much longer. He was assigned the tremendous task overseeing the installation of electric lights in Philadelphia, New York, London and many other major cities. In 1890 he wrote a book revealing the intricate details of electric lighting entitled, "Incandescent Electric Lighting: A Practical Description of the Edison System." Lewis Latimer was responsible for numerous helpful inventions and innovations before his death in 1929.

George Washington Carver
Born: January 1864
Died: January 5, 1943

GEORGE WASHINGTON CARVER

George Washington Carver was born a slave on a plantation in Missouri in 1864. He was kidnapped along with his mother by slave-raiders during the Civil War. After a long search, George was the only one recovered by his owner, Moses Carver. Carver exchanged his prize horse as ransom for the boy's return. George lived with the Carvers for many years after the incident. At some point the boy taught himself to read. Growing up in rural Missouri, he developed a love for various wild plants in the forest surrounding the Carver plantation. When slavery ended, the boy stayed with the Carvers a while longer until his desire for a real education emerged. George traveled west and spent the next twenty years working hard and preparing to enter college. In 1887 he enrolled at Simpson College. While there he was encouraged to pursue his artistic talent in art. Though he showed great promise in that area, George was more interested in having a career in science. After leaving Simpson in 1891, he entered Iowa Agricultural College where he earned a B.S. degree in 1894 and was recognized as one of the college's outstanding scholars. George also accepted the offer to become the first black man to serve on that faculty. He taught agriculture and bacterial botany. And during his tenure at the school he pursued a master's in research and experimentation. George developed plants that were more disease resistant than the old plants. His work became so well known, Booker T. Washington sent a request for the scientist to come to teach at Tuskegee Institute. When he was told how desperately his black people needed him, George went to Tuskegee Institute to teach. His scientific farming instructions did improve the productivity of land, especially that of the local sharecroppers and farmers. George spent the rest his life teaching and spearheading many agricultural research projects there at the Institute until his death in 1943. The results of his discoveries and inventions won him great acclaim among agricultural chemists as well as scientists from other countries. Three hundred products from the peanut and one hundred eighteen products from the sweet potato were developed by Carver during his years at the Institute.

Matthew Henson
Born: August 6, 1866
Died: March 9, 1955

MATTHEW HENSON

Henson was born August 6, 1866 on a farm that had been used as a slave market in Najemay, Charles County, Maryland. After the death of his parents, Henson eventually found his way to Baltimore, Maryland where he took a job as a dishwasher in a restaurant. Over-hearing the exciting accounts of patrons' foreign adventures, the thirteen-year-old was inspired to sign on the Katie Haines, a ship bound for Hong Kong. For six years Henson traveled the world. In those years he visited China, Russia, Africa, and Japan and some other countries as well. He learned the customs and languages of some countries. When the captain grew fond of Henson he became his mentor and taught him many important skills. Those important skills such as navigation, seamanship, mathematics, and geography really proved to be quite beneficial during his subsequent adventures. They actually turned out to be lifesaving. Six years later after the sudden death of the captain, Henson returned to Washington, D.C. where he took a job in a clothing store. Shortly afterwards in 1887, Henson was introduced to Lieutenant Robert E. Peary, a civil engineer with the U.S. Navy. The nineteen-year-old eagerly accepted an offer to go to Nicaragua with him as his personal assistant. For more than twenty years the men took many trips together. They made several Polar expeditions before becoming co-discoverers of the most northern part of the earth, the North Pole in 1909. Henson became an expert at Arctic living. His mastery of particular skills during his early adventures made him essential to the team. He was the only one that learned Inuit, the language of the Eskimo and Henson made sure they had all the things needed for survival during their extended stay in the Arctic. On April 6, 1909, after the team reached the Pole, Henson raised the American flag on the spot. However, when the men returned to the United States, Peary was the one acknowledged for the great accomplishment. Peary never revealed Henson's contributions. In 1912, Matthew Henson wrote the book, A Negro Explorer at the North Pole. Sadly, his accomplishments were not recognized by Congress until 1945, at which time he was finally awarded a silver medal for bravery. He died in 1955.

Jesse Owens
Born: September 12, 1913
Died: March 31, 1980

JESSE OWENS

Owens was born to struggling Alabama sharecroppers Emma and Henry Owens in 1913. He was the last of eight children. He suffered serious health problems, the effects of recurring pneumonia and other ailments. When the family move to Cleveland, Ohio following the great migration of Southern blacks seeking a better life, Jesse was then nine years old. Upon entering Fairmount Junior High School, Jesse's athletic talents were recognized immediately by Charles Riley, a teacher and coach at the school. Riley recruited the boy and began training him as a runner and a jumper. Jesse set a new junior high world record in the broad jump and in the high jump. Then in high school, Jesse set a broad jump record in sophomore year. He was among the top finishers in the 100 – and 200- yard dash events at the 1931 state scholastic meet. He dominated the state meet by tying the record for the 100 -yard dash and winning the broad jump and 220-yard low hurdles as a junior, then as a senior, the world scholastic record for the 100-and 220-yard dashes and the broad jump. In 1935, he set new records in five events that resulted in him being chosen in 1936 for a spot on the U.S. Olympic Team heading to Berlin, German. Winning gold in the 100- and 200- meter dash events, the 400- meter relay, and the broad jump, Owens was the most outstanding track star in the Berlin, Germany Olympics. He proved that Hitler's racist propaganda that German athletes were of a superior race was a fallacy. Owen became the world's fastest runner. However, his accomplishment was not acknowledged by Hitler. And sadly, some writers say, his accomplishment was not acknowledged by the President of the USA either. When Owens returned to the States he retired from the track racing circuit. Then he was unable to get decent paying employment. And sometime the jobs offered were quite demeaning. One such job required him to race against a horse. After moving to Phoenix, Arizona in 1972 his life changed for the better. He was also awarded an honorary degree from Ohio State University.

Rosa Parks
Born: February 4, 1913
Died: October 4, 2005

ROSA PARKS

Parks was born Rosa Louise McCauley in Tuskegee, Alabama on February 4, 1913. She grew-up in a broken home that was headed by her mother, her grandmother and grandfather. At an early age she was exposed to the evils of racial injustice. She went from being just an ordinary citizen in the city of Montgomery, Alabama to becoming one of the major players in the Civil Rights Movement because of the bold stand she took against such in the South. Of course, the response was quite harsh, but not a surprise to the forty-two-year-old grandmother. Growing up in Pine Level, Alabama, she was certainly familiar with the southern practice of segregation and prejudice experienced by her family and other blacks from most white land owners, overseers, and public officials. The South's Jim Crow Laws made it lawful to treat Black Americans as second-class citizens. In 1955 Mrs. Parks was taken to jail for refusing to give up her seat on a Montgomery city bus to a white man though she was not sitting in the white section. She was charged with breaking the local segregation law. A fellow member of the NAACP came to her rescue. After being bailed out of the jail, the news of the arrest caused her to lose her job. Serving as secretary of her local NAACP branch for years, Mrs. Parks had worked on similar civil rights projects before. She used her time in preparation to boycott the bus company by making phone calls, setting up car pools, and getting people to donate money for the cause. Another organization circulated thousands of fliers calling for a boycott, and the local Black preachers put the word out from their pulpits. Not everyone, black or white felt that a boycott would end well for Blacks. They feared reprisal from the white community. The boycott caused the bus company to lose so much money, it went out of business. And after a year- long boycott, the United States Supreme Court struck down Alabama's Jim Crow Laws. It was deemed illegal and unconstitutional in these United States of America. Rosa Parks was regarded as the "Mother of the Civil Rights Movement". In 1996 she was awarded the nation's highest civilian honor, the Medal of Freedom, given by President Bill Clinton. She died at the age of 92 on October 4, 2005 in Detroit, Michigan.

Granville T. Woods
Born: April 23, 1856
Died: January 30, 1910

GRANVILLE T. WOODS

Granville T. Woods was born on April 23, 1856 in Columbus, Ohio. He left elementary school at ten years old to work in a machine shop. He never returned to complete a formal education. Nevertheless, Woods did pick up many skills that he used later in his career. At the age sixteen he migrated to Missouri and got work as a fireman and an engineer on the railroad. After studying electrical and mechanical engineering Woods secured employment as an engineer on the Danville and Southern Railroad. It was during his time there many of the ideas used in his later inventions were born. He produced so many useful devices, he became known as "the Black Edison". The phrase was meant to honor and equate Woods' creative genius to that of Thomas Alva Edison's. Many of his inventions greatly improved the safety and efficiency of the railroad. Still in use today, is the third rail which provides electrical power to trains as they travel on the rails. He also devised a system for sending telegraph signals between trains while they are in motion to prevent accidental collisions. By the year 1880 Woods had obtained 22 patents, but not without challenges. The Thomas Edison Company filed a claim indicating the railway telegraph system had actually been invented first by Edison. Woods had proof that he was the original inventor of the system for which the company claimed. He had other patent disputes in court with the Edison Company. Woods won by proving he had patents to his inventions, but legal fees depleted most of his income. Many of the devices invented by Woods were purchased by such large companies as the Edison Electric Company, the American Bell Telephone Company, and Westinghouse. Because few had done more in the field of electricity and railway safety during his time, Woods was said to be the "Greatest Electrician in the World". After his death in 1910, records showed more than sixty patents assigned to the name of Granville T. Woods.

Harriet Tubman
Born: 1821
Died: March 10, 1913

HARRIET TUBMAN

Tubman- was born a slave on a plantation in Dorchester County, Maryland about 1821. By eight years old Harriet was working in the fields as well as in her master's home. She was often beaten if her owners were dissatisfied with anything she did or did not do. At the age of thirteen, Harriet was accidentally struck on the head by an iron weight while attempting to intervene in the punishment of another slave by the overseer. The accident caused her to experience life-long blackouts without warning. After a long period of recovery, she was sent to another plantation where she met and married John Tubman, a paid field worker, not a slave. Deciding to seek freedom also, Harriet tried to get her husband to leave the plantation with her when she was ready, but he refused. A very determined Harriet Tubman escaped by going north at night through miles of unknown territory. At twenty-five, Harriet was free. However, she could not be truly happy knowing there were so many others still slaves. She joined the Underground Railroad, a network of safe houses and anti-slavery activists, to help others escape. Time and time again, Harriet led risky rescue missions to bring slaves to freedom. Her final trip in 1857 included her parents for whom she assumed complete responsibility. To her credit, more than three hundred slaves were brought to freedom. After a large price was placed on her head, she was forced to go to Canada just before the Civil War started. But in 1862, she returned to the United States and became a spy for the Union Army and helped to save the lives of many wounded soldiers by nursing them back to health. Her concern for others did not end when the war was over. Harriet continued her benevolent activities in the interest of the less fortunate. Those activities included raising funds to support schools for former slaves, collecting clothes for the needy, and giving assistance to the disabled. Harriet Tubman died on March 10, 1913 in Auburn, New York at the age of ninety-three.

Benjamin Banneker
Born: November 9, 1731
Died: October 9, 1806

BENJAMIN BANNEKER

Banneker became one of the most famous Black Americans during the late 1770s. He was born on a farm near Baltimore, Maryland in 1731. His father was a slave, and his mother was a free woman. Because Benjamin was born of a free mother, he was free also. His parents encouraged him to study hard so that his future would be a success. He did not disappoint them. At a young age he preferred reading books rather than the usual playing. Fascinated by a pocket watch given to him, he invented a wooden clock after learning how the watch worked. Completed in 1753, the clock kept perfect time and would strike every hour. It is said to have been the first clock ever to be built in the United States of America. His favorite subjects in school were mathematics and the science of astronomy. Benjamin excelled in mathematics, however eager to learn as much as he could about both subjects. After leaving school in eighth grade, the lad continued his quest for knowledge. He became particularly interested in making mathematical calculations relating to the stars and the constellations. From an old astronomical table found in a borrowed book, he was able to make accurate calculations to predict solar eclipses and other phenomena related to the heavens. His interest in the sciences led to writing and publishing of his own almanac. It became a popular reference for farmers living in the Mid-Atlantic areas. His great accomplishments did not go unnoticed after a copy of his first almanac was sent to the Academy of Science in Paris by Thomas Jefferson. For ten years afterwards, Banneker continued to published his almanac. Concerned about the slave situation, many of his articles were in opposition to the institutions of slavery and war. In 1771 Benjamin Banneker was commissioned by President Washington to assist in surveying and planning the layout for the District of Columbia. Just as it is today, the layout of streets and the major buildings are a monument to Banneker's genius. He died at home October 25, 1806.

Bessie Coleman
Born: January 26, 1892
Died: April 30, 1926

BESSIE COLEMAN

Bessie Coleman was the first black female pilot. She dreamed of opening an aviation school to train blacks and women in particular, to fly airplanes. After moving to Waxahachie, Texas from Atlanta, Texas to sharecrop cotton, the family fell on hard times when their father left to return to his Choctaw roots in Oklahoma. To make ends meet the children were expected to pitch in. Bessie being the youngest, was not able to do hard jobs so she was assigned to help out doing white people's laundry. In 1917, Bessie went to live with an older brother who was a veteran of World War I. Hearing his stories involving fighter planes fueled her dream of flying planes. Landing a job as manicurist in a Chicago barbershop gave Bessie the opportunity to listen to other soldiers tell about their war experiences. Fascinated by their accounts of women flying planes in France, Bessie set out to learn French and to secure finance for aviation lessons in France, the only place such studies were offered to blacks or women in 1920. In 1921, Bessie Coleman received an international pilot's license, the first ever to be awarded to an American woman or any black American by the Federation Aeronautique Internationale. Though putting an end to the prevailing myth that blacks and other minorities were less capable of flying planes, Bessie was unable to obtain employment or get finance to start an aviation school in the states. Disappointed, she returned to Europe. Once there, she took advanced flight training and secured employment as a test-pilot for famous clients, one in particular, the world-famous acrobatic stunt performer called the "Flying Dutchman". With Bessie's reputation soaring as an accomplished pilot, she decides to pursue a career performing acrobatic stunts. Her amazing acrobatic maneuvers thrilled spectators and were often captured on film. She then decides to return to the U.S. and perform her flying exhibitions and give lectures around the country in an effort to raise capital to start her school. Her first engagement was in 1922 at Curtiss Field near New York City, sponsored by the Firestone Rubber Company. In 1926 Coleman and her mechanic were killed when the plane she rented malfunctioned during a trial run before her May Day performance in Jacksonville, Florida.

Althea Gibson
Born: August 25, 1927
Died: September 28, 2003

ALTHEA GIBSON

Gibson- was a trail blazer in the sport of tennis. She was the first African-American to break down the racial barriers that existed to keep black athletes from competing against whites. Althea's amazing talent in sports was recognized on the streets of Harlem by her peers before her rise to fame. She was challenged often to compete in basketball, shuffleboard, badminton, or paddle tennis. Enthusiastically, she accepted and made a formidable opponent. Eventually, her unusual talent caught the attention of a local PAL supervisor who took her to the Harlem River Courts to be matched with more experienced players. Her extraordinary performances led to the offer of professional lessons from a prestigious black tennis club. During the 1940s, sponsored by the all-black American Tennis Association, Althea became a local success. After she had won several Women's ATA National Championship titles her sponsors decided that the time was right for her to compete nationally in the sport reserved for the white. In 1950, Althea Gibson was entered into the Indoor Championships sponsored by the U.S. Lawn Tennis Association. Though she won first place in the Eastern indoor Championships and second place in the National Indoor Championships, her victory was never acknowledged until a former champion exposed the USLTA's racist actions to a leading magazine. Althea went on to become the world's number one female tennis player in the fifties. She won the French Open, Wimbledon, and the U.S. Open Singles titles in 1957 and 1958. After dominating the women's world of tennis, Gibson joined the Ladies' Professional Golf Association in1963, and was appointed special consultant to the New Jersey Council Physical Fitness in Sports in 1988. Gibson published her autobiography, "I Always Wanted To Be Someone", and years later she published her second book, "So Much To Live For".

Henry Ossawa Tanner
Born: June 21, 1859
Died: May 25, 1937

HENRY OSSAWA TANNER

Ossawa Tanner grew up in Philadelphia, Pennsylvania where his father was a Methodist minister. It was thought he would become a minister as well, but Tanner dreamed of becoming a painter. His parents allowed him to attend the Philadelphia Academy of Fine Arts to pursue his dream. After graduating in 1880, Henry took a position as an art instructor at Clark University in Atlanta, Georgia until deciding to follow a new dream, to study abroad. Paris was his choice of residence. An illness made his return to the U.S. necessary to recuperate in 1893. It was during that time he painted two compositions, "The Banjo Lesson" and "The Thankful Poor". The paintings were barely acknowledged by the art world at that time. Tanner had dared to stray from the usual stereotyped characterization of Blacks portrayed in American art. Even some African-American critics felt that Tanner should use his talent to develop an African-American style that would give rise to a "School of Negro Art". Bewildered by the prevailing racism in America, Tanner returned to Europe where his new paintings depicted scenes of a religious nature. They received wide acclaim. The French government's purchase of Henry's "Resurrection of Lazarus" for the Luxembourg Museum was a great honor, one of many received by him. Some of his other masterpieces include "Daniel in the Lion's Den", "Christ Walking on the Water", "Moses and the Burning Bush", "The Disciples on the Road to Bethany", "The Two Disciples at the Tomb", "The Disciples of Emmaus", "The Flight into Egypt", "The Scapegoat", "Christ and Nicodemus", "The Repentance of St. Peter", and "The Immaculate Conception". There were other religious compositions painted as well. The black artists influenced most by Henry Ossawa Tanner, thought of him as a true genius. He made Paris his home where his work received recognition in the fine arts without a bias to nationality or race. In Paris he was free to produce the kind of art he wanted to create. When Henry Ossawa Tanner died in 1937, his death was truly a great loss to the art world.

Marian Anderson
Born: February 27, 1897
Died: April 8, 1993

MARIAN ANDERSON

Anderson, a Philadelphia, Pennsylvania native, was encouraged to pursue a singing career. Her amazing talent was recognized at an early age. As part of her church involvement she often sang with both the junior and the senior choir groups because of her ability to sing multiple parts and ranges. After hearing her beautiful contralto voice, Roland Hayes, a singer of classical music, told Marian, she should be singing Mozart and Beethoven, and that she had the chance to be great. He suggested professional coaching for her. But since her family did not have the money to spend for lessons, the black church community gave concerts to raise the funds to help get the training she needed from local professionals. In high school Marian was accepted as a student by instructor Giuseppe Boghetti who taught her classical songs and arias. She practiced and worked hard knowing her success depended on it. Her efforts paid off when she was entered in a competition held by the New York Philharmonic Society as one of three hundred contestants. As the winner, Marian's prize was an appearance with the New York Philharmonic Orchestra. While her performance was magnificent, she received few engagements because of the racial biases that existed in the United States. Realizing the situation, her manager took her to Europe where she worked with many leading musicians. It was during her many travels and performances there she received some of her greatest compliments and honors. Anderson, remembering the struggle of African-Americans in the fine arts, established the Marian Anderson Award in 1942 to benefit young singers that chose the same path. In 1943, the now renowned singer was given the opportunity to sing in Constitution Hall. She also became the first African-American to sing on stage at the Metropolitan Opera House in 1955. In 1956 she wrote and published her autobiography, "My Lord, What A Morning". Marian Anderson gave a farewell concert in Carnegie Hall in 1965, and was one of the world's five most esteemed contraltos to receive the first John F. Kennedy Center honors in 1978.

Jackie Roosevelt Robinson
Born: January 31, 1919
Died: October 24, 1972

JACKIE ROOSEVELT ROBINSON

Jackie Robinson was the first Black American to play baseball in the major league. He became one of the greatest players of all time. What an achievement for one whose life started out on a sharecropper's farm in Cairo, Georgia! After Jackie Robinson's father deserted the family, his mother moved her family to Pasadena, California, determined to give her children the chance for a better life. When the boys got old enough to work, they contributed to the family's income. Delivering neighborhood newspapers was Jackie's first real job. During High School he participated in baseball, track, football, and basketball. He excelled in each sport. And later, at Pasadena Junior College he set a new world record for the college in broad jump, and was named the most valuable junior college player in southern California. Later, after entering UCLA, Jackie Robinson became the college's very first student to ever earn varsity letters in four sports. In 1945, Robinson returned home after serving in the U.S. Army as a moral officer. His experience was not a happy one due to racism that existed in the Army. He found a job playing professional baseball for the Kansas City Monarchs of the Negro National league. Jackie Robinson's talents, courage, and discipline caught the attention of Branch Rickey, president and general manager of the Brooklyn Dodgers. Rickey was looking for someone who had the guts to help break the color barrier in Major League baseball. To the dismay of many, Branch Rickey signed Jackie Robinson as a member of the Dodgers on April 10, 1947. Though Robinson received many racial insults and threats from some coaches, fellow teammates, and white fans of baseball, he remained focused on the goal to help bring down racial barriers in all team sports. He went on to earn the Rookie of the Year award in 1947 and the Most Valuable Player award in 1949. During his ten seasons with the Dodgers he led the team to six pennants and one World Series Championship. After retirement from baseball, Robinson got more involved in the civil rights struggle. He became the first African-American to be inducted to the National Basketball Hall of Fame.

Langston Hughes
Born: February 1, 1902
Died: May 22, 1967

LANGSTON HUGHES

Hughes was named James Langston Hughes by his mother Carrie L. Mercer at birth on February 1, 1902. Though born in Joplin, Missouri, Langston lived in many places while growing up. He was very lonely and unhappy. Reading character adventure books and writing poetry became a welcoming escape for him. When the boy got older his father, James Nathaniel, a black businessman, offered him college tuition to become an engineer. In 1921, Langston entered Columbia University in New York City for a short time, then dropped out to pursue a different path. After trying a series of jobs, he became a seaman on voyages to Europe and Africa. After learning Spanish and French, Langston lived for long periods in France, Spain, Italy, Mexico, and Russia. However, New York is where his literary genius was recognized and further developed. Langston Hughes became a leader in the Black Arts Movement of the sixties and was often referred to as the "Shakespeare in Harlem" and the "Poet Laureate of the Negro Race" because of the extensive body of literature written and translated by him. His own work chronicled largely the difficult lives of his race of people. His technique of using African-American vernacular in his writing was initially seen as unproductive by many of his contemporaries and was not embraced by the lot. But it was not long before his technique became popular with them all. Three poems most famous for Langston's technique are "The Weary Blues", "Fine Clothes to the Jew", and "Ask Your Mama". Langston Hughes, one of the most honored authors in America lived in New York City until his death in 1967.

Frederick Douglass
Born: 1817
Died: February 20, 1895

FREDERICK DOUGLASS

Douglass was born a slave in 1817 in the backwoods of Maryland's Eastern Shore. At an early age he was hired out by his owner to work for a family member until he passed away. Douglass was then returned to his master and passed on to Hugh Auld, the brother of the slave master. Fortunately, this time he got the opportunity to learn to read and write. However, when Hugh Auld discovered his wife giving their son and Frederick literacy lessons, he sternly reminds her of the laws against teaching slaves to read. He told Mrs. Auld that such would make a slave unfit for slavery. From that point on, the boy began learning secretly and reading abolitionist texts and discussing the ideas of freedom with others. A change in the youth's attitude did not go unnoticed by Hugh Auld. He felt that Frederick was beginning to display behaviors unbecoming a slave, so he decided to send the boy back to his brother's plantation. To teach Frederick a lesson Thomas Auld hired the boy out to Edward Covey, a notorious slave breaker. Extremely harsh treatment from the slave breaker caused the youth to rebel violently. In 1836 Douglass escaped to freedom with the aid of friends and found refuge in New York, and later in Massachusetts. He changed his last name from Bailey to Douglass so he would not be found by the old slave master. Douglass joined the Massachusetts Anti-Slavery Society which sponsored his travels throughout New England speaking about the evils of slavery. He had to hurriedly leave the states after publishing a best seller, his first autobiography, *"The Narrative of Frederick Douglass"*. Thomas Auld went to court and demanded the return of his slave, Fredcrick Douglass. A year later, the British Anti-Slavery Society presented Frederick Douglass with papers to prove he was a free man. Once back in the states, Douglass founded a newspaper in Rochester, New York called The North Star. It dealt with the issues of slavery until President Abraham Lincoln issued the Emancipation Proclamation. Frederick continued his fight for the freedom of his people right up to his death on February 20, 1895.

Booker T. Washington
Born: April 5, 1856
Died: November 4, 1915

BOOKER T. WASHINGTON

Washington was born into slavery near Hale's Virginia about 1856. His mother, Jane was a plantation cook; his birth father was unknown. At a young age Booker was made a house servant until slavery was abolished after the Civil War ended in 1865. Washington's mother then moved her family to Malden, West Virginia to join her husband, Washington Ferguson. At nine, Booker T. joined his stepfather in the salt and coal mines where he worked. In the evenings the boy taught himself to read and write. By fifteen he had saved enough money to attend Hampton Institute, at that time a trade school. After enrolling he took the job as janitor. The hard work that he committed to did not prevent his graduating with honors in 1875. After teaching in Malden briefly, Washington was asked to return to Hampton to teach there. In 1881, he was sent to Tuskegee, Alabama to establish Tuskegee Institute. Washington believed that vocational schooling was a real necessity for Blacks to obtain financial and economic stability, and to build their character. Under his leadership the Institute soon became the leading school of its kind for Black Americans. However, some people were not pleased with its vocational focus. Many educated Blacks saw its curriculum as insufficient and lacking in preparation for students to compete for equal opportunities as whites. And some southerners did not want Black Americans to receive any education at all. Booker T. Washington became a prominent national leader among Black Americans. He traveled throughout the states making speeches, developing groups of Black businessmen, and securing financial supporters. Before his death in 1915, Washington was often consulted on race issues by white leaders in politics and was awarded many honorary degrees. He also wrote 14 books; included his autobiography, "Up From Slavery", first published in 1901.

Thurgood Marshall
Born: July 2, 1908
Died: January 24, 1993

THURGOOD MARSHALL

Marshall was named to the Supreme Court by President Lyndon B. Johnson in 1967. He became the first Black American to serve on the highest court in the land, making him one of the most important lawyers and judges of the twentieth century. Years before serving the highest court in the land Marshall was made a federal judge by President John F. Kennedy in 1961 and four years later, named Solicitor-General of the United States by President Johnson. Thurgood Marshall was born July 2, 1908 in Baltimore, Maryland a racially segregated city. After earning a law degree in 1933, Marshall started his own law practice in his home town. He began to use his legal expertise to fight the injustice in his city which were many. Known as a staunch advocate for the rights of individuals, the National Association for the Advancement of Colored People asked him to join them in their fight against racism. Marshall became their busiest lawyer. There he continued his fight against injustice. As the chief counsel for the NAACP, he headed their legal defense fund, and traveled from state to state defending legal cases for Blacks and acting as a civil rights ambassador. One of his memorable battles was the case of "Furman verses Georgia." He influenced the Court to overturn Georgia's procedures used to impose the death penalty. Marshall took a hard stand against the practice of capital punishment because he felt it was meted out unequally. He saw this as a violation of the constitutional provision against cruel and unusual punishment. Marshall skillfully used the Constitution to force state and federal courts to protect the rights of Black Americans. He became a national hero in 1954 when in the case of "Brown vs. Board of Education" the Supreme Court ruled segregation in all public schools unconstitutional. For years afterwards, Thurgood Marshall was referred to as "Mr. Civil Rights" because of his refusal to compromise when the rights of the poor and disenfranchised were threatened or violated. Many cases handled by him brought about significant changes in our society. He died in 1993, but will long be remembered as a protector and defender of the underdog.

Martin Luther King, Jr.
Born: January 15, 1929
Died: April 4, 1968

MARTIN LUTHER KING, JR.

Martin Luther King was born in Atlanta, Georgia on January 15, 1929. He grew up amid the influences of a father who was the pastor of a church. Years later, King was ordained a minister and elected assistant pastor where his father served. King's concern regarding unjust southern racial practices made him eager to learn how past philosophers dealt with social problems. He went to Crozer Theological Seminary. There he learned about Mohandas K. Ghandi of India who used non-violent methods to free his people. After leaving the seminary, King enrolled at Boston University where he earned a Doctorate, and also met his wife Coretta Scott. After leaving Boston, King became the pastor of the Dexter Avenue Baptist Church in Montgomery, Alabama. Shortly after King began his ministry in Montgomery, Mrs. Rosa Parks was arrested for refusing to give up her seat on a bus to a white man. When King and other Black leaders heard the news, they agreed to boycott all the buses in the city. For an entire year every African American that depended on the buses, walked or drove to work. Not only did those bus companies go out of business from loss of revenue, the Supreme Court ruled Alabama's bus segregation law unconstitutional. That meant the law of segregation was illegal. Sit-ins, marches and demonstrations were organized to publicize this peaceful fight for freedom. On August 28, 1963, the March on Washington led by Dr. Martin Luther King, Jr. gave new importance to the Civil Rights Movement and exposed the evils of racism to the world. In 1964 Dr. King became the youngest person to ever receive the Nobel Peace Prize. He used the prize money to help further the fight to eradicate discrimination against black Americans. He was an important leader until his assassination in Memphis, Tennessee on April 4, 1968.

Ida B. Wells-Barnett
Born: July 16, 1862
Died: March 25, 1931

IDA B. WELLS-BARNETT

Ida B. Wells-Barnett was born into slavery on July 16, 1862 in Holly Springs, Mississippi. She became an early participant in the fight against racial injustice as an adult. James and Lizzie Wells were her parents. James was the companion and also the son of their slave owner. When President Lincoln issued the Emancipation Proclamation in 1862 freeing the slaves, James and Lizzie chose to stay in their old jobs. Ida was their first born of the seven children. Education was a priority for the Wells. The children were enrolled in a school run by Northern missionaries. However, Ida's final year in high school was interrupted when her parents and youngest sibling contracted yellow-fever and died in 1878. Ida assumed the responsibility of caring for her siblings while continuing her education as well. She eventually accepted a teaching job in one of the black schools in Memphis, Tennessee. Ida Wells activist side emerged in 1884 when she was forced to give up her first-class seat on a train to a white man for one in the smoking car. She resisted and was put off at the next stop, but not before biting the conductor. Back in Memphis, Ida filed a lawsuit against the railway company and won. Then the decision was reversed by the Tennessee Supreme Court. Disappointed that the law did not assure justice for everyone as she believed, Ida would continue to fight such injustice toward Blacks. She acquired a part interest in a black newspaper call Free Speech. As editor of the paper she had the freedom to challenge issues blacks faced such as the separate but not so equal schools, the lynching of innocent black men, the hiring of poorly educated teachers to staff black schools, and job discrimination, etc. Ida Wells-Barnett spent much of her life fearlessly battling against discrimination and risking her life to expose the truth. Her actions decades earlier influenced the civil rights movement of the 1960s.

Madame C. J. Walker
Born: December 23, 1867
Died: May 25, 1919

MADAME C. J. WALKER

Walker, the daughter of former slaves, developed the first hair care products for black hair. Her business success made her the first African-American female millionaire in the United States. At birth she was actually named Sarah Breedlove. She was born December 23, 1867 on a Louisiana plantation. Her family worked in the Burney family's cotton fields until both parents died from yellow fever. When Sarah and her siblings were unable to manage the work they moved on to look for similar employment in other towns. At fourteen, Sarah married Moses Mc Williams and had a daughter named A'lelia in 1885. Two years later when Sarah was widowed, difficult times caused her to seek work in St. Louis, Missouri as a cook and a laundress. When her hair began to fallout, she mixed up a concoction that she claimed to have dreamed of in her sleep. After significant signs of hair growth appeared, the hair product was then tried on friends with good results as well. Sarah then began selling her product door to door until deciding to move to Denver, Colorado to set up a business there. Months after moving, Sarah married Charles Joseph Walker, a newspaper sales agent. Taking his name, she called herself, Madame C. J. Walker, and her product Madam C. J. Walker's Hair Grower. Their use of available advertising in black newspapers was helpful in promoting sales. Eventually, the pair traveled to parts of the eastern and southern states to expand their hair care business. In 1908 the Leila College to train hair culturists was established in Pittsburgh. And after setting up a headquarters in Indianapolis in 1910, Madame Walker had a factory built, a beauty school, and a hair salon. Later a laboratory was constructed for the purpose of the research and the development of new products. Business flourished in the USA and beyond its borders. While Walker's successful business ventures made her a wealthy woman, it gave those that were employed by her the opportunity to make a decent living. She employed twenty thousand workers in the United States and in the Caribbean. Madam C.J. Walker participated in various social and political organizations in an attempt to bring about positive changes in the African American community. She died in 1919.

James P. Beckwourth
Born: April 6, 1798
Died: October 29, 1866

JAMES P. BECKWOURTH

Beckwourth, a legendary figure was born in Fredricks County, Virginia in 1798. He was the son of a slave woman and a white slave owner. When young James was about seven, the family relocated to St. Louis, Missouri. At fourteen, his father sent him to serve as an apprentice to George Caster, a white blacksmith. Because of Caster's strict rules, a violent confrontation took place resulting in James making a hasty departure, never to return home. He got work in a salt mine. That ended in 1823 when he met General William Henry Ashley and his group of fur- traders in St. Louis, heading west. James Beckwourth joined the group. From that day forth Beckwourth's life was a series of adventures. He helped the fur-traders bargain with the Pawnee Indians for horses to travel the rugged terrain of the Rockies, hunted for the expedition's food supply, and learned to trap beaver. He enjoyed living life as a frontiersman. During his life time, he traveled extensively and was even adopted by the Crow and served as their chief for six years. After participating in many battles and adventures with them, he left to look for new adventures. In 1850 Beckwourth made a very significant discovery while crossing the Sierra Nevada. It was a pass through the mountains which gave settlers a way to reach California and the Pacific Ocean. This gateway proved to be an influence in the opening of the West. James Beckwourth himself led the first wagon train through it. Later, Beckwourth Pass became a route used by the Western Pacific Railroad. The name of the pass is still recorded on American maps today. James Beckwourth, one of America's greatest black explorers and frontiersmen died in 1866.

Sojourner Truth
Born: 1797
Died: November 26, 1883

SOJOURNER TRUTH

Sojourner Truth was born into slavery in 1797 on a farm in Ulster County, New York. Isabella Baumfree was her given name. After being bought and sold by numerous slave owners she was forced to marry an older slave. When her children were taken and sold to other slavers by her own master, she ran away. When she discovers that her only son had been sold after the passing of New York's emancipation law in 1828 freeing all slaves in the state, Sojourner Truth presented her case before the magistrate and won his return. Unfortunately, the search for her other children were not as successful. Her search was long before she was able to connect with any of her daughters but she never gave up. Sojourner's employment as a servant in New York City gave her a taste of freedom, but she wanted much more. She began to travel throughout the country spreading God's word and speaking out against slavery. Even though it was outlawed in some parts of the country, it still existed in other places. Though she could not read or write, she had a keen intellect that drew others to listen to her. She spoke also for women's rights and dedicated a great part of her life helping slaves. While Sojourner was not part of the Underground Railroad network she encouraged many to use it as a means of reaching freedom. Her goal was to help them live better lives. When she grew too old to continue her crusade, she moved closer to her daughters living in Battle Creek, Michigan. She died there on November 26, 1883 at age 85. Sojourner Truth became the most famous African American woman during her time. Before her death she was recognized for her dedication and service by President Abraham Lincoln.

Daniel Hale Williams
Born: January 18, 1856
Died: August 4, 1931

DANIEL HALE WILLIAMS

Daniel Hale Williams was born on January 18, 1856 in Hollidaysville, Pennsylvania. He was one of seven children. When his father died, Daniel was ten years old. Life for the Williams changed drastically and money was limited. His mother moved to Janesville, Wisconsin with relatives. Daniel was left with a family member to continue his education. After completing high school, he travelled to rejoined his family in Janesville. He tried various jobs, but was dissatisfied with them because his real desire was to attend medical school to become a doctor. With the help of a barber friend he was hired in the office of the Surgeon General of the State of Wisconsin. And after two years of hard work and study, Daniel passed the entrance examinations to attend the Chicago Medical College. He earned his M.D. Degree in 1883 and then did an internship at Mercy Hospital in Chicago, Illinois. Dr. Dan as he became known, opened his first office in Chicago and was on the surgical staff of several institutions where he taught anatomy. In 1891 Dr. Williams organized a group of prestigious African-American and White doctors to establish the Provident Hospital and Training School Association. Before the medical association African-American doctors usually had to perform surgeries in the homes of their patients. Existing hospitals refused to appoint Blacks to their staff or train black nurses. With Dr. Williams as surgeon the school became the first of its kind in the U.S. Then more blacks were able to be trained as nurses and nursing assistants. Dr. Daniel Williams perform the first open heart surgery that was ever successful. The procedure required great skill and daring. The amazing result was reported in all the newspapers and medical journals. The doctor was honored by being elected a Fellow of the American College of Surgeons in 1913. Till this day he is still regarded as one of America's greatest physicians.

Percy Lavon Julian
Born: April 11, 1899
Died: April 19, 1975

PERCY LAVON JULIAN

Percy was born in Montgomery, Alabama on April 11, 1899. He was the eldest of six children. His dream was to become a chemist despite serious obstacles he might face. That industry was known to be out of reach to Black Americans. Nevertheless, Percy was determined to follow his dream. He had been taught very early by both of his parents the values of a good education, hard work, and persistence. With eighth grade completed, Percy enrolled in a teacher training school to get the equivalent of a high school education since no further schooling was provided for Blacks. Upon being accepted at DePauw University in Greencastle, Indiana in 1916, he chose to work in the area of chemical research. But because of his weak former educational training he was required to take an additional two-year course of study. After all the hard work, Percy ended his four years of college as class valedictorian. However, he was unable to land that preferred industrial job suitable for him. He accepted a job as a chemistry teacher at Fisk University. In need of a fellowship to continue his education, Percy applied to Harvard. He was accepted and from there earned a Master's Degree. He then went to teach at Virginia State College for a year until he was asked to return to Harvard to develop a laboratory. After enrolling in the University of Vienna to pursue additional studies, Percy receives his Doctor's Degree in 1931 after which he returned to the States to start a scientific project at Harvard, then returning to DePauw at the college's request to work in its research department. Finally, Percy Julian got an industrial job with a company in Chicago. The company required his expertise to experiment with soybeans for which he found many uses. The research led to the discovery or several synthetic substances which can be used in paint to make it water tight, a drug called cortisone, which alleviates the pain caused by arthritis, and a foam that was used to smother fires during WWII. It saved the lives of many sailors and soldiers. In 1954 he set up his own laboratories, then merged with a Philadelphia Pharmaceutical firm in 1961.

Jan E. Matzeliger
Born: September 15, 1852
Died: August 24, 1889

JAN E. MATZELIGER

Matzeliger was born in Paramberio, Dutch Guiana in South America on September 15, 1852. As a child he developed a passion for machines and watching ships go out to sea. When he got older his father allowed him to work in his machine shop along with him. Jan was fascinated with all the machines and what they could do. He became really excited to learn how to use the lathe machine that cut and shape metal. He spent much of his leisure time on the dock watching the big ships sail in and out to sea. His dream of sailing away on one of those vessels one day, was very much alive. When Jan finally realized his dream as a seaman, he was nineteen years old. He sailed to the Far East. In 1873, two years later, his ship docked in Philadelphia, Pennsylvania. Trying to get employment in a factory was hard for Jan. Though slavery had ended ten years earlier, many white business owners would not hire Blacks for factory jobs. Finally, his job hunt came to an end when he was hired by a shoemaker. He began his job by learning to use the Mckay machine that sewed leather together to make the soles for shoes. Jan was so impressed he wanted to learn more about making shoes. In 1877, Jan relocated to Lynn, Massachusetts where he was hired at the Harney Brothers' factory as a shoemaker's apprentice. He liked all the different machines used to make the finished shoe. Nevertheless, in time he felt that it took too much time to produce such a limited number of shoes. Ignoring the doubt and the mockery of his fellow workers, Jan set out to develop a shoe-lasting machine that could perform multiple jobs, increase shoe production, make shoes fit better, and make them more affordable for everyone. At last, the job was done! He designed a machine that shaped the upper shoe leather over the last and attached it to the sole of the shoe using tacks. Matzeliger patented his lasting machine on March 20, 1883. Eventually, a large company purchased it, and many other companies throughout the world began using it to produce more shoes than ever before. Today, Jan's invention has been improved, but it remains the same in principle.

Carter G. Woodson
Born: December 19, 1875
Died: April 3, 1950

CARTER G. WOODSON

Woodson was the oldest of nine children born to former slaves. He was born on December 19, 1875 in the small town of New Canton, Virginia. After receiving a substandard education at the elementary school level, the boy was sent to work in the coal mines of Huntington, West Virginia to help support the family. During the evenings Woodson continued a course of study on his own. It wasn't until 1895, at the age of twenty, he finally enrolled at Frederick Douglass High School. His remarkable academic performance earned him a diploma after only two years. After pursuing a brief teaching career in West Virginia and receiving a degree from Barea College, Woodson's interest changed to traveling and studying abroad. In 1912, Woodson was only the second African American in history to earn a Doctorate Degree from Harvard University. In 1915, Woodson and several of his associates formed the Association for the "Study of Negro Life and History" to encourage an in-depth study of the Black past. He became seriously concerned about others distorting African and African American history. And he believed that most of the information obtained came from missionaries, travelers, and bureaucrats which he felt were not reliable sources. To counter the disparaging portrayals of Blacks, Woodson and the association distributed carefully chosen Black History books as textbooks throughout the Washington school system. The books were prepared for elementary to the university. Woodson was the principal founder of Back History Week, the catalyst in popularizing the teaching of African American history in schools nationwide. (In 1976 it became Black History Month.) Dr. Woodson wrote and edited many books and articles. The following are a few of his published books: A Century of Negro Education; History of the Negro Church; The Rural Negro; Education of the Negro Prior to 1861; Miseducation of the Negro; African Backgrounds Outlined; and The Negro in Our History.

Wilma Rudolph
Born: June 23, 1940
Died: November 12, 1994

WILMA RUDOLPH

Rudolph was born in Clarksville, Tennessee on June 23, 1940. She was one of twenty-two children. During her early years she was afflicted with scarlet fever, double pneumonia, and polio which left one of her legs paralyzed and in need of a leg brace. Therapy was required on a regular bases for approximately two years. Her inability to participate in physical activities with other children caused Wilma to become depressed for a time. When she had fully recovered, her father encouraged her to get involved in sports at her high school in Clarksville. She chose basketball and track. She was one of the best basketball players in the state, averaging over 32 points per game. And in track she was a sensation. Her hard work and determination resulted in her becoming an undefeated sprinter in every high school track meet. She went on to win the state sprint titles at 50, 75, and 100 yards. In 1956 Wilma Rudolph, at the age of sixteen went to her first Olympics in Melbourne, Australia. There she won a bronze medal as a member of the women's 4x100-meter relay team. Then in 1960, Rudolph became the first American woman to win three gold medals in track and field at a single Olympics. And because of her unique running style, she was dubbed by the crowd of onlookers "la gazella nera" (the black gazelle). When Wilma Rudolph retired from running in 1962, she returned to college to get a teaching degree and also continued to work with youth. In her later years, she established the Wilma Rudolph Foundation to help youngsters obtain an education and training as athletes. Wilma received many honors and awards during her career as well as in her retirement. In 1984 The Women's Sports Foundation selected her as one of America's five greatest women athletes of all time. She was inducted in the Women's Sports Hall of Fame, the Black Sports Hall of Fame, the U.S. Olympic Hall of Fame, and the National Women's Hall of Fame. Her Autobiography: Wilma; The Story of Wilma Rudolph was published in 1977 and adapted for a television movie. She died on November 12, 1994 at her home in Brentwood, Tennessee.

Ernest Everett Just
Born: August 14, 1883
Died: October 27, 1941

ERNEST EVERETT JUST

Ernest E. Just was a brilliant pioneer in the field of biology. He was born in Charleston, South Carolina to Charles Frazier and Mary Matthews Just on August 14, 1883. His experiments in cell research provided an important breakthrough for treating many serious diseases. Since cells are the building blocks of all living things, his findings revealed their functions. This significant discovery made possible more effective treatment of such life-threatening maladies as cholera, smallpox, and bubonic plague. These serious conditions have been eradicated from civilized society, and many others have been considerably checked as a result of the biologist's extensive cell research. However, his findings and ideas were not readily embraced by the scientific community, acceptance occurred gradually. Just's keen intellect was evident in his earlier years. After the untimely death of his parents, a school teacher, enrolled him at Kimball Union Academy, a white institution in New Hampshire. There he excelled in his studies, and was elected to the Phi Beta Kappa Academic Society. Upon completing the Academy's four-year academic program in three years, Just was accepted at Dartmouth College. He was selected as a Rufus Choate Scholar for two years straight after earning the highest marks in Greek at the college. In 1907, he graduated magna cum laude, and was awarded special honors in zoology, history, botany, and sociology. That same year Ernest Everett Just was hired to teach biology at Howard University where he was head of the Department of Zoology until his death. His vacations were spent with noted biologists who met at the Marine Biological Laboratory at Woods Hole, Massachusetts to study the fundamental biological problems concerning the cell. By 1915 he was the leading contributor to biological journals and widely quoted on such matters as fertilization, artificial parthogenesis, cell division, hydration and dehydration in living cells, etc. Even before Just earned a Ph.D. from the University of Chicago in 1916, he was on his way to establishing his reputation. And before his death in 1941, his reputation had been firmly established for years in the scientific world.

Phillis Wheatley
Born: May 8, 1753
Died: December 5, 1784

PHILLIS WHEATLEY

Wheatley was the first African American to publish a book of poetry. At the age of about seven or eight the youngster was kidnapped from her native homeland in West Africa and sold into slavery in 1761. A well-to-do merchant purchased her from a Boston auction block to be a maid for his wife and daughter. She was formally educated in her master's household by his wife, Susanna Wheatley and their daughter, Mary. They instructed Phillis in grammar and religion. Within months the child was fluent in English and was reading classics from the Wheatley library. Shortly, she began writing beautiful rhymed poetry about friends and events that concerned her Boston circle. In 1767, when Phillis was fourteen years old her poems appeared in print for the first time. To determine the authenticity of her work, Thomas Jefferson had it evaluated by leading intellectuals of that time. In 1770, she wrote a mournful poem of lament to commemorate the death of the English evangelical George Whitefield. It got attention throughout the Atlantic world. As a result, Phillis gained the friendship and support of Countess Selina Hastings who had the influence to get her poems published in London, England. So, impressed with the girl's poetic skills and expression of emotional feelings, the countess encouraged Phillis to complete her book, Poems on Various Subjects, Religious and Moral. Since the countess was at the center of the anti-slavery Methodist circle, she was eager to use the writings of former slaves as evidence against slavery. Phillis' literary success refuted the notion held in Colonial America that slaves were incapable of higher intellectual thinking. After the book's publication in London in 1773, Phillis Wheatley was hailed as a prodigy. But she never got a chance to make her presentation to the British court. She was ordered to return home to care for Susanna who had become seriously ill. After Susanna's death, Phillis was given her freedom. Even though she continued writing poetry, her life changed considerably when she lost connections with previous contacts she had made while living with the Wheatleys. Before her death in 1784, she had slipped into poverty and obscurity.

Paul Laurence Dunbar
Born: June 27, 1872
Died: February 9, 1906

PAUL LAURENCE DUNBAR

Dunbar was born in Dayton, Ohio on June 27, 1872. His parents were Joshua and Matilda, once slaves in the state of Kentucky. Neither parent could read or write until they were freed, and taught themselves. At the age of four, Matilda taught Paul to read. When the boy started school, he was far ahead of his class. He would read books even when it was time to play. In high school, he was president of the literary society and editor of the student newspaper. The Senior Class graduation song was also composed by him. When Paul's father died during his high school term, his plan of becoming a lawyer was over. Paul had to help support his mother. He helped deliver laundry, then he became an elevator operator after graduation. Occasionally, Paul would submit an original poem to his local papers. Then Paul Laurence Dunbar's literary genius really began to flourished. Dunbar became the first Black American of the early nineties to receive national acclaim as a poet in the states. Initially, his use of black dialect in his work caused some of his contemporaries to feel it promoted negative stereotypes of black lives. Nevertheless, Dunbar continued his style. Eventually, a group of men of literary stature took an interest in Dunbar's work. Though he wrote classic English verses also, he is known best for his lyric dialect poems. His interpretation of black life appeared in his first book, Oak and Ivy in 1893, and then better expressed in his second one, Majors and Minors in 1895. While humorous, his poetry evoked the suffering, the hope, the tragedy, and the triumph of the Black spirit oppressed by racism. Those two books of poetry gained Dunbar much recognition in the literary world. He published additional volumes of work, became a popular lecturer, and gave poetry readings. Paul Laurence Dunbar was extended an invitation to go to London to recite his work at Queen Victoria's Diamond Jubilee. And back in the United States, he was acclaimed as the "poet laureate" of the Negro race. Dunbar experienced great success before his death in 1906.

Garrett A. Morgan
Born: March 4, 1877
Died: July 27, 1963

GARRETT A. MORGAN

Garrett A. Morgan's birthplace was Paris, Kentucky. He was born to former slaves Sidney and Elizabeth Morgan on March 4, 1877. Garrett was one of eleven siblings. At the early age of just fourteen with only an elementary school education, he moved to Cincinnati, Ohio. Because of his meager education he was only able to get employment as a general handyman for a white landowner. Morgan left Cincinnati for Cleveland, Ohio after a few years because the lack of other opportunities for him. After teaching himself about sewing machines, he got employment as a machine adjuster with a number of companies. In a few short years he was able to purchase his own shop that sold and repaired sewing machines. His success led to his opening a tailor shop in 1909. It was during that period Morgan developed a chemical hair-straightener which was marketed as the G.A. Morgan Hair Refining Cream. It is thought by some to be the first of its kind. In 1912, Morgan invented a mask he called the gas inhalator that was later called a gas mask. After obtaining a government patent for it in 1914, that same year he received the first prize gold medal for his mask at a safety and sanitation fair in New York City. For years afterward Morgan's mask was used to save the lives of firemen, policemen, soldiers, and other workers who came in contact with smoke or poisonous gases. After some improvement, the mask became standard equipment for U.S. soldiers on the battlefields. His creative genius surfaced again when he invented the first traffic-light system to prevent the increasing automotive collisions on the streets. The rights were bought by the General Electric Corporation. Today's traffic signals grew out of Garrett Morgan's invention. Before his death in 1963, he was cited by the U.S. Government for inventing the first traffic system.

Elijah McCoy
Born: May 2, 1844
Died: October 10, 1929

ELIJAH MCCOY

Elijah McCoy was born in Colchester, Ontario, Canada on May 2, 1844. His parents fled Kentucky two years before his birth to escape from slavery. Elijah received his early education in Ontario until the age of sixteen. His secondary education took place in Scotland where he studied drafting and engineering. After the training, Elijah became a master mechanic and engineer and decided to migrate to Ypsilanti, Michigan, now that slavery had been abolished in the states. He was not successful finding a job in his field due to the prejudice that still existed against blacks in the United States. Elijah settled for jobs as a fireman and an oilman for the Michigan Central Railroad. The work was very hard. It required shoveling tons of coal into the train's firebox to produce steam to keep the train running. He also had to lubricate the machinery with oil by hand every few miles to keep the train running smoothly. Elijah, realized there was wasted time when the train stopped to be lubricated. He invented an automatic "lubricator cup" to do the job in 1872. It delivered oil to all the parts that needed it. He received a U.S. patent that same year. When the Michigan Central Railroad finally tried Elijah's invention, it worked so well other companies want it also. Some even made attempts to duplicate it, but none worked as well. Those companies that wanted the original would request "the real McCoy." The same expression is still used today when referring to "the real thing" not a copy, nor a fake. The lubricator cup was Elijah McCoy's first invention. In 1882 he became a full-time inventor. He received fifty-seven patents for his inventions, most were for oiling heavy machinery. In 1920, the inventor formed the Elijah McCoy Manufacturing Company in Detroit, Michigan. McCoy died in Detroit, Michigan on October 10, 1929.

BIBLIOGRAPHY

Amram, Fred M.B. African-American Inventors. Capstone Press. Mankato, MN. 1996.

Kathryn I. African American Heroes and Heroines/150 True Stories of African Americans Heroism. Lifetime Books Inc. Hollywood, Florida. 1998.

Bracks, Lean'tin. African American Almanac/400 Years of Triumph, Courage and Excellence. Visible Ink Press. Canton, MI. 2012.

Falstein, Mark. Meeting the Challenge. The Continental Press, Inc. Elizabethtown, PA. 1987.

Fouche, Rayvon. Black Inventors in the Age of Segregation. The John Hopkins University Press. Baltimore, Maryland. 2003.

Gates Jr, Henry Louis, et al. The African American Century: How Black Americans Have Shaped Our Country. Simon and Schuster. New York, N.Y. 2002.

Gates Jr, Henry Louis. Life Upon These Shores/ Looking At African American History: 1513 --- 2008. Alfred A. Knopf a division of Random House, Inc. New York and Canada. 2011.

Gates Jr, Henry Louis, et al. The African Americans/ Many Rivers To Cross. Smiley Books and Hay House, Inc. United States. 2013.

Gates, Karen Grigsby, et al. African American Voices of Triumph/Perseverance, Time-Life Books Inc. Alexandria, Virginia. 1993.

Haber., Louis. Black Pioneers of Science and Invention. Harcourt Brace Jovanovich, Inc. San Diego, California. 1970.

Hamilton, Virginia. Many Thousands Gone/African-Americans From Slavery to Freedom. Scholastic Inc. New York, N.Y. 1996.

Hodges, Norman E. W. Black History. Monarch Press. New York, N.Y. 1971.

Klein, Aaron E. The Hidden Contributors: Black Scientists and Inventors in America. Doubleday and Company, Inc. Garden City, New York. 1971.

Lanker, Brain. I Dream A World /Portraits of Black Women Who Changed America. Stewart, Tabori and Chang. New York, N.Y. 1999.

Lyman, Darryl. Great African-American Women. Jonathan David Publishers, Inc. Middle Village, N.Y.1999.

Rogers, J.A. World's Greatest Men of Color, Vol. II. Macmillan Publishing Co., Inc. New York, N.Y. 1972.

Smallnud, David, et al. Profiles of Great African Americas. Publications International, LTD. Lincolnwood, Illinois. 1998.

Stevenson, Lisbeth Gant. African-American History/Heroes In Hardship. Cambridgeport, Massachusetts. 1992.

ADDITIONAL RESEARCH RECOMMENDATIONS

Historical Figures
Richard Allen
Isaiah Dorman
Estevanico
Jean Du Sable
Robert Smalls
Charles Chesnutt

Scientists and Inventors
Henry Blair
George Carruthers
James Forten
William Hinton
Norbert Rillieux
Lloyd Augustus Hall

Leaders and Politicians
Ralph Bunche
Shirley Chisholm
A. Philip Randolph

Military Figures
Benjamin Davis, Sr.
Henry Flipper

Writers and Artists
Sterling A. Brown
Zora Neale Hurston
James Weldon Johnson
Jacob Lawrence
Richard Wright

Educators
W.E.B. Du Bois
Charles H. Houston

www.ingramcontent.com/pod-product-compliance
Lightning Source LLC
Chambersburg PA
CBHW081505070526
44586CB00019B/2491